maybe some day it might make sense

Luis Feliciano

BookLeaf Publishing

India | USA | UK

Presentation by *BookLeaf Publishing*

Web: www.bookleafpub.com

E-mail: info@bookleafpub.com

ISBN: 9789358311334

First edition 2023

To my partner, Kristen Hoffman. May our art continue to grow together.

To my parents, Eileen Figueroa & Luis Feliciano. Without you, I would be nothing.

ACKNOWLEDGEMENT

Thank you to BookLeaf Publishing for giving me the opportunity to actually try and do something artistic.

PREFACE

This a bunch of poems I put together, with less thought than someone like Rupi Kaur, but surely with more effort than a sloth.

always better than someone else

I'm in London:

I heard a black man say to a black woman,
"You're just poor."
The words dripping off the tip of his lips

The titanic submarine imploded
And I care more about those 5 people,
Than over 750 refugees being lost in the
Mediterranean

In America,
I sing songs from a musical,
"Everyone's a little bit racist"

I laugh because it's true
And now I realize I'm classist too

I'm always judging

not sure

i keep letting go of parts of myself

that i really thought i needed, but i don't.

like, caring so much about how I sound when I
sing

In fact, when I come down on myself about it, I
do worse — …

I hate writing sometimes

because with the words on the page it's so
obvious

being mean to myself makes me shrink

when I get out of the way

I am more free

Time Apart

We are spending our time apart, growing in our
own ways

And I can't tell if I'm growing away from you

Or I see the truth more clearly now than I ever
have before:

The truth of who you are, the person you want to
be versus the person you really are

a new rhythm

I feel mountains moving inside me

My psyche shifting tectonic plates

causing my bones to quake, my heart to skip a
few beats: finding a new rhythm

choosing

5

sometimes I feel like I reach out to the world,
and my messages just arrive into the ether

into space, basically

But Space would be a better place for my woes

Than this emptiness between us

Where I feel like people see

And then,

Choose: to ignore

summer '23

French clowns

American cowards

Spanish cooking

WORDS: THE NEWEST CRAZE

I wonder what it was like back when words
mattered less

Like, when it was a new discovery

And there were people hating on it, like

Bah bah bah, those will never catch on

oof

i didn't come all this way

for my experience to be ruined

by strangers, and dumb luck

Kristen, my love

I want to give you the whole wide world

and buy you a dress with pockets big enough to
carry it.

//

When I think of traveling, I think of it with you

When I think of eating, I think of what you
would like

When I think of acting, I think of what your
perspective would be

--

I never thought my wildest dreams would come
true:

Being with someone that has the same hopes and
dreams

And the same will and drive to get it all done

~~

I'm nervous thinking about you reading this

Because I feel like no matter how much I write, I
won't be able to capture the effect you have had
on my life

And the love I have for you in my heart, in my
soul

For now, we just keep watching TV in this weird
9th floor apartment in Paris

agada agada agada

always easier said than done

to stay consistent

committed to my art work

I feel like giving up all the time

just settling into a life of teaching undergraduate
students things they couldn't care less for

sticks and stones

i came all the way to France

to have this old man say mean things to me

But you know,

it's quite better than

being lied to all the time

winding down

I'm trying to figure out how to wind down at
nights

I feel like I'm just getting started when everyone
else is going to sleep

~~~ finally

No more distractions
~~~

nightmare fuel

I had this nightmare that I would keep having to
leave to go return this car at the airport but for
some reason it would just loop back to playing
this video game that I HAD to complete before
leaving, but it wasn't a perfect loop, because I
would start with less time each time until by the
end I would be getting to the airport with 30
minutes left, and I've been down that path
before, running running running to the gate

goddamn i can't stand being late

precious little words

my relationship to words, goes like this:

I am either doing personal writing in a journal,
that no one ever reads

Or

I read non-fiction pieces on theatre, on acting
techniques mostly, sometimes how to direct

NEVER, reading fiction

or writing from a perspective that is not my own

And, being a (quite good) math teacher,

I also spend time meticulously choosing which
words and which order of them makes math
make sense

SO:

When I go on stage and I'm supposed to have
fun with words,

I freeze up.

To me, right now,

Words are no laughing matter

Not something to be shrugged off and ignored.

But I see, that not a lot of people agree

They say shit just to say it sometimes,

Just because that arrangement of words makes a
funny

ha ha

ha

fun (haiku)

I need not force fun

I can let myself have it

again and again

the lie of the internet (very selfish)

we lie to each other on the internet all the time

yes, literally, of course, that's obvious

What I mean now is similar to what is happening
with this book:

I pretend that I am speaking to you right now

And you are pretending the same

We are somehow in a "connection" here

though I have no idea when you're reading this,
or what part of the world you are in, whether I'm
even still alive to know

and you may even be having the profound
experience of feeling less alone in the world

but I didn't write this for you.

I wrote it for me.

And you aren't really reading for me,

You're reading for you, and what you might get
out of it.

When I write I feel release

and it still feels good whether anyone receives it,

or not. (very selfish)

oh dear

I can't sleep any more

I had a dream that my parents did the
unthinkable... (divorce)

And the worst part about it,

they were actually happier apart.

tea break

For years, I have had tea most nights

At some point, I even started having some in the
morning

And, slowly, starting having some through out
the day

during small breaks, long breaks, any break at
all really

And now, suddenly in France, there is no tea

(or rather, I'm not letting myself buy any)

And I am starting to have just the wildest,
wildest dreams

scientifically, they say, I'm catching up on REM
sleep

spiritually though, I feel like I am processing
years worth of subconscious brain activity

positive and negative feelings I suppressed

Because it was so much easier to just have tea.

too good to be true

oof, we're starting to get to the end here

Im getting a little paranoid that I won't actually
make it

Even though we've come so far

Don't you get that feeling too?

too precious

oh dear,

i'm getting too precious

it's almost over

and now all of a sudden i'm in a deep pit of
despair

how do i close this thing out

it's got to mean something

leave a lasting impression, no?

and so it went

here we are

right at the end

I'm getting emotional

Mostly anxious

What if I never publish again

What if I never actually make a living wage off
of acting

What if I never work with people who I can
learn from

sigh

I'm sorry I'm not better at lying

www.ingramcontent.com/pod-product-compliance
Lightning Source LLC
La Vergne TN
LVHW051247200726
843510LV00011B/1733